The Sun Behind the Sun

Adrian Rogers

The Sun Behind the Sun

The Sun Behind the Sun
ISBN 978 1 74027 860 7
Copyright © text Adrian Rogers 2014
Cover image © INFINITY – Fotolia.com

First published in this form 2014
Reprinted 2015

Ginninderra Press
PO Box 3461 Port Adelaide SA 5015
www.ginninderrapress.com.au

Contents

One	9
The train – high summer tyranny	10
The Kassam Pass – a New Guinea dreaming	12
Port Broughton in two modes	14
Night train	16
Two	17
Mambray Creek dreaming	18
Between and beyond times	19
Long-ago school – the alien world	20
Called	22
Three	23
from Four Seasons – Autumn acceptance	24
Sunset reflectivity	25
Night into dawn	26
Illusions observed from a moving train	27
The night coach	28
Four	29
Stranded boat	30
Sonic track in time	31
What was and is…	32
The last spark	33
Night drive	34
Five	35
Descent of the Logos	36
Camper's dawn	38
Alone	39
One more venturing – a sea dreaming	40
The night walker	41

Six — 43

- Timeless deconstruction — 44
- Papering the cracks — 45
- Reflections on time – 1 — 46
- Reflections on time – 2 — 47
- Night voyage — 48

Seven — 49

- Encounter – a street dream — 50
- The pendulum — 52
- Vigil — 53
- Fire — 54
- Holograms — 55
- Time stopped — 57

Eight — 59

- Stopped — 60
- Subtractions of winter — 61
- Expectation and uncertainty — 62
- Howard Springs (near Darwin) – a landscape fantasy — 63
- Spring equinox — 65

Nine — 67

- Off the tracks of time — 68
- Intimate promenade — 69
- Time and the cat — 70
- The swallowing twentieth century — 71
- Summer solstice — 72

Ten — 73

- St Kilda — 74
- The switch-on — 75
- The life voyager's beacon — 76

A love speculation	77
Autumn equinox	78
Eleven	79
Sea images	80
The image of touchdown	81
Commuters break the mould	82
Australian landfalls	83
Winter solstice	84
Twelve	85
Migrant	86
Perception of an echo	88
The Shell	89
Changes	90
Spring Tides	92
Epilogue	93
The sun behind the sun	94

One

The train – high summer tyranny

High summer sun
hammers
this anvil of a station platform
where I am caught
as concrete and bitumen
hurl back
their unstored heat.

Foot soles are
superfluously warm
and bare legs sting.

February midday
over forty
is a scorching flail
endured…until
metal on metal's
slide and hiss
is a train rolling in.

Doors thud open
and conditioned air
coolly exhales
a welcomed
temporary respite
from hazed-over glare
and light-heat tyranny's
aggregation
soon to be lost
when 'journey's end'
is the long rolled-out
metallic pulses
ceasing again
for my return
to hammer and anvil…

another station platform.

The Kassam Pass – a New Guinea dreaming

A skeletal crash barrier
curved starkly deformed
rearing above a drop
as from the head of the Pass
the highlands fell precipitously

the slopes
densely dark green glittering
wetly leech-like jungle
sweeping untamed
infinitely downwards
into a vapour-smoking morning

the sun glared over-whitely hazed
and evaporation
was the forest's incense
rising from distant depths
like chanted sorcery

a descending serpentine
hard-built highway
unwound across the mountain's edge
like the caduceus of Mercury.

We stopped
and skewed with relief our glances
to mellow-green variegated
sun-sheened lowlands
made magical by distance
and impressionistic finger lines
of patchwork cultivation
ashimmer overall,
but before this paradise fantasy
could be regained and tamed
a wavelike wild traverse
of height and depth intensified
by imaginations run amok
was a driver's unavoidable initiation
into outcomes of weathering
on a road running past
its use-by date.

Port Broughton in two modes

Mode 1 – tidal moods

A branch-like arm of land
curves, sweeps
enclosing a charm
of ebb-flow waters slow
like white glass burning
under midday sun
or ripple/stippled steel grey
minimally restless
when weed flavoured breezes
stir sluggish seas
beyond illusory dodge tides
only to lapse back
into mirroring shorelines
jetty piles and boats
imaging a concentrated calm
in shallowness yet with
sentient depth
of dreaming beyond
soundings, endings
and beginnings.

Mode 2 – the bite swarm alliance

Foot-stirred seaweed
bakes in enervating
breeze deprived heat
releasing black biting
sand fly swarms
like remembrances of tasks undone.

Never do today
what you can put off till tomorrow

is the mantra as mosquitoes
blend, a swarming alliance.
Again the bite
but less obtrusive
apart from niggling
whining unwanted reminders of

never do today
what you can put off till tomorrow.

Low tide mud flats
echo bird calls
hazed sky their sounding board.
Boats huddle
confined to a narrow
far-side-of-the-bay channel.

Never do today
what you can put off till tomorrow.

Time from the starting blocks
is running,
holiday beginnings
and endings
trip over each other
till one becomes another.

Never do today
what you can put off till tomorrow

until tomorrow is today.

Night train

In sleep
you have no destinations
suspended above
the sotto voce iron music
of wheels on rails
only the dream unquiet
filling empty spaces
no past or future
beyond half believing hopes
slumped across seats and luggage
or prone in compartmented
semi-comfortable illusions
low lit
against night's infinitude
where darkness is
a 'Cloud of Unknowing'
beyond down drawn blinds
another country, mystery
of timeless emptiness
though a train may stop
severing dream connections
islanding you anywhere
in breathing silences
of endless moments,
but what lies
beyond the unperceived
is unknown.

Two

Mambray Creek dreaming

(Alligator Gorge, South Australia)

From a dry stone creek bed
pale, bark-peeling trunks
stand up
flinging skeletal branches
against an unmarked sky
their backdrop a looming
eroded, cracked gorge wall
red-brown behind struggling bushes
demanding living space
despite the breaking stone.

Half grey olive-green
haphazardly cascading leaves
betray the presence
of an unseen water source
as a breeze rattles
tough leaf clusters
their upper faces exposed
to an inquisitorial sun.

Birdcalls counterpoint
the wind song
but what are they saying?

Between and beyond times

Between two waves
eternity is
the measureless moment
a gap between breaths
a silence of awe
a motionless wait
and immeasurably
the dying fall
of a foam flecked
curl-topped transitory hill
through a cosmic cyclical
returning.

Long-ago school – the alien world

He stands
at the class's head
with serried brown ranks
of scored, polished desks
defining serried grey ranks
of boys in shorts
with blazers part red
and ties striped accordingly
calling names from the register.

'Answer when
called!'
he says
'I should have thought it was obvious'
he thinks
'to answer your summoning'
but I ponder instead
desk-incised names
of the long-departed
boys known only
by inscriptions on wood
speaking across silence
as definers of time endured
between walls
enclosing this present space
wherein I sit
alienated now.

Can nothing supersede
the embattled moment,
no voice from elsewhere
while I strive still to recall
that lost inarticulate cry
of birthing,
another world
and time?

Called

After an episode in Rose Macaulay's novel *Towers of Trebizond*

Dawn...
as light burned off the water's surface,
hands net tangled pulled
and bodies leaned
against a struggling weight of fish
as distant mountains shaded
towards powder blue
before an ordinary day hardened.

Did they catch a silver-meshed sun
chafing against vision disturbed routine
run counter
to the grain of suitability
for what might be
drop nets and leave
because of The Word,
reject the backward glance
eat the Salmon of Knowledge
barefoot tread stone paths

walk with stars?

Three

from Four Seasons – Autumn acceptance

Cooled ripe richness
Keats' image
in the place time defined
English evocation
is not here
where autumn's
attenuating actions
of light, temperature
fruit, bark, branch and leaf
discriminate equally.

Towns rooted elsewhere
may sport imported theatrical
turned-red growth, gold, russet
under a weakening sun,
alternatively
slackening heat grip
dawn-evening sharpness
and blown leaf patterns
against bright off-white skies
say what is needed.

Winter mists may be
pale day greyness
beyond slatted blinds
but ripple-fluted
shakuhachi magpie magic
is enough
on the winding
towards winter track
fearing no seasonal desiccation
into age.

Sunset reflectivity

A track of light crosses water
ambiguously gold-silver
pink tinged shimmering
pale foot muffling sand and weed
in grey anonymity
contrast a glimmering
beneath thin cloud strands
ink-dark, streaked red
against a simmering
sun-gold ball diminishing
between breaths slowed down
into vanishing.

Night into dawn

From night into dawn
inner-spaced eternally
dream vanishing residues
and emerging hopes
intersect
between falsehood, truth
dark and light at star-fade
and that sky wide grey tinted
long night's ending
timelessly staging
the Morning Star's rising
before the sun.

Illusions observed from a moving train

(Near Elizabeth Station)

Illusion
is larger than life
and darkness
the belief enhancer
that nothing is
as it is.

Traffic lights
fleetingly, like dropped
Christmas illuminations
conspire magically
with distance eluding
tomorrow's back-flip
into yesterday's memories
until reality
'tomorrow never comes'
is glimpsed in passing
captured between eye-blinks
as a green belt slips
beyond the train
and desire
imprints the idyllic
moment coloured image
surface reflected
window divided
greener
for being untouchable.

The night coach

A night ride's interrupted dozing
is boredom punctuated
by the muffled
rolling sound-smother
of rubber on bitumen
cabined, dim-lit
for would-be sleepers
turning heads
against seat backs
position changing
bolstering illusions
of comfort, and hopes
to shorten time enclosed
against a world
of vanished horizons
and the endless dark,
until cold transfers
inharmoniously break
time's slow stretched
yet timeless patterned
sleep snatched moments
on the ride
towards a dawn's
hopeful insecurities
through unstructured tales
of 'Night Ride and Sunrise'
a rite of passage
into new beginnings.

Four

Stranded boat

Wet sand stranded between tides
like someone slumped over a bar stool,
in line a swift grace image
for the curved
white collared wave onrush
impatient with idleness
your sweeping bow
snubs, challenges
provocative breezes
to hear
sun-painted
salt-breath-scoured
the welcoming flood.

Sea road lifting
aerial gulls salute
as you rise again to wind song.

Sonic track in time

The voice untracked
single purposed
pursues inflected
to notational edges
disciplined free chant
stone light crossed
gold sung through arches
echoes, voyages
among dancing dust motes
alchemically three times seven
times like Hildegard's dove
in flight among
and beyond the spheres.

What was and is…

pain is like a line along the tide's edge
imprinted
like a watermark on sand
like foam trapped between seaweed
and wave-shaped ridges
lingering…like seashore flotsam
banked, abandoned by the ebb
unforgettable
until time's flood heals
like the sea's smothering
of what was, and is.

The last spark

Time passes
like thread-thin incense smoke
or someone stepping forward
out of the almost dark,
leaf-stripped shadow trees
cast across sunset-angled light,
and the last spark scatter
from the last smouldering log
is caught
'in memoriam'
afterwards, like transference
on an outward breath
the 'Ground Luminosity'
against black night rising.

Night drive

Sleep is your enemy
depersonalising
on the long unwinding road
scattering perceptions
of time's passing
when night
has swallowed the horizon
constricting you
in spaces digitally lit
by numbered dials
and signal blinks
while scything headlights
challenge vainly
the unconquerable
starlit and moon-white
glowing dark
so beware the lurk
of lotus-eating haunters
on the road to paradise
'don't text and drive'
they will subsume
your microcosmic world,
close out their penetrating
soft enticing tiredness
one breath
from loss imponderable
surrender never
to 'A Charm of Lullabies'.

Five

Descent of the Logos

Tired evening
road dust settling
a donkey's head drooping
as the winch rope creaks
dry sounding
as a man draws water from the well –

'Aye, 'twas slow day-long going through crowded ways.'

The weathered stranger moves on
undaunted by the prospect
of a house not home
merely a birthing place, knowing
beyond this space time balance point
a god pillar will fall
when one family traverses the stone hard road
to Heliopolis and the Virgin Tree
caught in the thicket
of an age's cusp
like the prefiguring ram
with Sirius ascendant
and the Wheel turning
because the Way has descended
from star paths to take
that crossing over into time
after the small death
between mountain peaks
while netted fish
on the river's rise
herald a rending

of an alienating veil
the Logos immanent,
alchemy's transcendence
transmuting the past.

Camper's dawn

Waking
in a tent
with the wind dropped
and night's last breath
a skin cold touch
I am aware
of cyclic returns
as a half world wakes
at cock crow
and an open eye
is a shutter closed
on dreams,
but a curtain raised
on illusions.

Alone

Alone
on the cream/grey grit
of a dirt road
in wing-fluttering daylight
with wind-tossed barley escaped
through rust-wire fences,
rough stubbled paddocks
like unshaven faces
and gnarled weathered
dark green trees,
I am
completely
the seasonal landscape
wing-fluttering daylight
on an old dirt road
alone.

One more venturing – a sea dreaming

Unstated purpose in his eyes
takes rhythmic light
sea and sky
into one movement's
reflexive touching of past futures
in weathered wood
a boat's sand-cushioned bow.

The sea calls
mind stirring discontent
with static earth
and wind whipped
soon-to-be-dropped sand
reality grounded
beneath a gull's wing.

Visions of distance
wrestle salt-sharp wind
wash over a mind alert
like waves against a sloping beach
their undertow-like lure
turning touch to grip
a long hull seaward thrust.

'Let the tide take her'
with dream-trapped Ulysses
'beyond destinations
to the withdrawing hem
of sea and sky.'

The night walker

Night-veiled, not alone
tap through the darkness
discreetly part the silence
stir no dust
aloneness
self-companionable
is alchemy
walking fearless into blackness
tap through the darkness
ghosts are companions
on the long night trek
beyond nemesis
tap through the darkness,
stir no dust
peripheral vision
is a vanished horizon
back into the future
forward to the past
beyond the world's end,
tap through the darkness
on the long night trek
fear is a dormant beast
couchant, unpredictable
but Nocturnes
are clouds, fetes, sirens,
almost silent dramas
so tap through the darkness
the Void is horizonless
but you are walking
towards the dawn,
tap through the darkness…

Six

Timeless deconstruction

Old house
deconstructing
stone
timelessly pitted
framed
wood-splintered decay,

a photograph?

Shattered
eyehole windows
witness
structured illusions
speak
soundlessly
as if risen
to abandonment
under impartial translucence
clouds
infinitely shaded
from grey
to grey
embedded
in consciousness.

To the land
return,
sky unfeeling
a magical mirror
is change
no change
leaving
the temporary image.

Papering the cracks

To keep
the sharp-edged vigil
is to reminisce yet
minimise an age
recalling
what was merely
a grounded structure
landscaped
into recollection
until, in desire's aftermath
nothing remains
before transmutation
but memory
papering the cracks
exposed by time.

Reflections on time – 1

How long is long
in the long slow
soundless drop
of the slow rotating shot
between tower walls?

Time is subsumed
in the gap
between air and water
as the shot
in freefall
globalises
between height and depth
before a dream-long
slow settling
consummation by water.

Reflections on time – 2

Time passes…

until the passing years
Time's unelected arbiters
possess the high ground
of our dreaming
while age creeps surreptitiously
on youth's conditional
taken-for-granted immortality
before the midlife equinox
after which
advantageous balances
are not always
shunted expeditiously
into autumnal sidings.

Flesh is
though diminished
still flesh until sublimated
by spiritually cathartic realisation,
a passion of waiting
on balanced returns
evolving subliminally
into sublimely
androgynous maturity
but with life having still
the last laugh.

Night voyage

A moon-white foam wake
froths fanwise
towards a vanished shore
your persona
left above the tideline
is no more than memory
the sea, impersonal
neither cruel nor kind
clusters mood phases
impartially distributing
scattered wrecks
non-judgemental
beyond cause and effect
like an albatross
ghost guiding the last ship
knowing no horizons to contain
a night sea voyager
crossing black water
star-sparked gold
moon pale-washed,
a state of being
between night and dawn
so let the sea rider
gaze-lift over
the world's end drop
where ending and beginning
never were, only the Void
a grounding all from nothing.

Seven

Encounter – a street dream

Deserted twilight street
a dream
framed stone and concrete
a step by step
resounding parade
of low-lit strangeness
and dulled lamps
a stranger approaching
detached
from silenced traffic
and leaves scattered
like confetti on pavement blocks…

bodiless
released from fleshly interference
elliptically enclosing
in the cosmic egg
insight
but not illumination
a 'being' state
because the Wheel has stopped
Prince and Beggar
cannot change economic places

neither going nor coming
he is…
the shot fall
between Centre and Zenith
suspended
imaging stopped time
beginningless, endless,
unheard but known
this unrevealing evening
movement and stasis
undifferentiated.

Who will re-start the clock?

The pendulum

At the swing mid-point
past is a present, future
no-state between times
and compass points
dream fluctuating
maximum and minimum
rhythmic melange

a timeless dodge tide
way-meeting point
one day
of a thousand years
and a nanosecond's
predictive motion
birth, dying,
the truth-weighed heart
at a swing mid-point's
night watch
between memory's past
present, future
mirth, sadness
resignation…

a pendulum
just is.

Vigil

Time is not
in the candle flame
a mountain-top moment

an eternal heart flicker
slow-pulsing aura
impinging on darkness.

From time released
a hermit's enclosure
is the heart's disclosure
in kaleidoscopic
time-out visions

A peopled blackness
All Hallows tryst
a shadow cast
by light beyond light
an offering for
loved ones revisiting
the eternal moment.

Knowing
All, beyond comprehension
light is…
from dazzling darkness.

Fire

Always
the unknown warrior's
strength, lion mastering
vigilance
reward
feeding the Eternal Flame
fire is
the elemental ruler
and a taper-lit invocation
to the Salamander.

No image
but unquenchable
flickering light
Agni – divine transformer
life beyond life
brought down and raised
star fire, supernova
and the gateway
is still
the Eternal Flame.

Tired eyes watch
faith kept beyond years
temple attuned
beyond time count
they – like the Pyramids
can laugh at time
theirs the light
perceived within…

the Eternal Flame.

Holograms

Evening winter light
on any street
time unspecified
a depleted
sun-shot overcast
is long-beam yellow
and insinuating shadows
slanting grey
across voiceless stone
concrete, and bitumen.

Footsteps return
from vanished years
echoing
through dull chilled air
remote
from elemental inspiration
framed
by silent looming buildings
and pavements uniformly
not quite deadening.

Street and shop
do not yet vaunt
their timed-out bright array
tempting materiality,
the Magician's staff upraised
has not brought down a charge
to vivify desire
only the stranger may confront
a dream's bilocating
semi-transparency
his voice tone flatly
self-projecting,
desireless…

'Reality self-perceives
the Wheel of Fortune
not redeemed by eloquence
but light
and mirror imagery
as holograms.'

Time stopped

When time stopped
springs unwound
a stone dropped
into a pool
ripples spread
dissipated
and the dust of history was undisturbed

silenced sound
was infinite mystery
a millstone ground
the last corn
life denial
saw no one born
and the dust of history was undisturbed

a muffled chime
was prophecy
a doggerel rhyme
proved entropy
a back turned
on progress
and the dust of history was undisturbed

affirmation
fired intensity
vision's confirmation
a propensity
for dreaming futures
and the Hermit
lantern-lit a path, then
the dust of history was disturbed.

Eight

Stopped

(Northern Ireland at any time during the 1970s)

Three shadows loom
beyond the windscreen,
waving arm wipers
on a rain-washed night
elbow water aside

STOP!

authority to search
throw calthrop on the road
impaling tyres
shoot if you decline
from the wrong side
of an orange/green
no white between border,
exiting
to rain flailing
yellow torchlight-painted familiarity

'Open the boot please!'
and wait
'Nothing here!'
'Thank you sir,' dispels ignored
fear vague undertows,
before re-entering,

driving
from disputations and desolations…

a border.

Subtractions of winter

Pared down
to a progression of winter days
one step at a time
detached, waiting,
in a fasting season
beyond strength unrenewed
and commitments unmet
one endures
like a predatory
ground shadowing kestrel
hovering as though
between light, shade,
a passionately illuminating hope
and the triangular interlock…

the wait continues.

Expectation and uncertainty

Veils
like stage curtains
or light switch dimmers
subtract definitive outlines
blurring a world circumscribed
enclosing, in haunted waiting
anticipated sight restoration
and another self-unveiling
tempered ephemerally
principally by uncertainty.

Should expectations denied
constrict circles of sight limitation
or should we affirm
the rose-fire transformation?

Howard Springs (near Darwin) – a landscape fantasy

Water like cool jazz
elucidates skin touch
sensualising subtly the life pulse
caressing the swimmer's twist and turn.

Light interactive illusion
belies like dropped diamonds
its heat source
scatters silver-white
intangibly dazzling surfaces
and separately
cosmos-in-miniature rainforest
breathes aromatic damp
gold/green shadows
and blue deepened
low reflections
under sleep-dazed flying foxes.

Beyond revelatory openings
into a spindly
dry grassed
overgrown landscape
scattered with tall askew
Carpentaria palms
sun-bright sky
dominates the rise
multi-oned birdcalls
mate with human
water-born shouts off-sprung
from frolicsome interactions
in light/water neighbourly
riotous harmony
masking the anarchic tread
of social change.

Spring equinox

Wind gusts
irrepressibly spring cleaning
water messages secreted
beneath grass and reeds
the Green Man looking down
through leaf-cascading branches
to the point of balance
equal night and day
is a moment eternal yet transitory
immediate, remote,
a here and gone
earth song fading
remembered, forgotten,
a bright green
shining overrun
unstoppable as bird song
self-renewing as birthing
realisation intangible
as mist, disappearing
like a passer-by
on 'The Long and Winding Road'
to summer.

Nine

Off the tracks of time

In a siding
off the tracks of time
weeds grow thick
between lines and sleepers,
rust of years
eats iron roofs
dry rot and rising damp
alternate
attacking woodwork,
engine roar
growl and strife of metal
are memories
ghostly echoes
of vanished lives.

Who will
roll back the silence
under a soporific sun
recalling
hands on stone
wood, iron
where the lizard basks?

Intimate promenade

In this room
are the pictures truly
'education by landscape'
or illusion
by flight from reality…
a pantheistic halfway house
guiding inviolate
individual pilgrims
along a path,
or a by-path?

Time and the cat

What is lost time
to the cat sunning herself
on a shed roof
or orchids spiking
in thin winter sunshine?

There's foot-tapping hardness
in rain deprived ground.

Are we declining
enduring
rapidly unfolding years
turning back into tomorrow
forward into yesterday?

The swallowing twentieth century

Animal Farm came and went
trains still run
and differentials seem ambiguous
after tax file numbers
swallowed undigested
century remnants
terminated in a loveless maze
of liberalised internet wanderings.

Must we
commercialise living and loving
hack maze-threaded
web-tuned lifelines
up a winding stair
or say 'a plague on both your houses'
we are what we are?

Summer solstice

Half-time called
in the seasonal game
and atmospheric layers
ozone depleted
mitigate the sun-fire
directly overhead
longest day heralding
shortened shadows
foreshadowing
a slow retreat
as the Green Man peers
defying drought memory
through green branches
at 'St John-in-Summer's'
ritual festive pace
knowing his fate
in time's foreshortening.

Ten

St Kilda

Sun glare and weekenders
a sharp edge of wind
off a winter sea
silver/blue patterning
light
without heat

sky surfing birds
calling above
sea grass at low tide

a cool jewel-blaze of brightness
and knife-keen perception
contrast
shadow and stillness
of primal mangrove
dreaming forests
above energised salt swamp
and moon-pulled tides

looking through
twisted green-flecked branches
over mud flats
and sun-polished water
to an engineered world
I observe
sediment to steel
continuity
through time.

The switch-on

After the Gnostic
intuitional 'switch-on'
is newness
landscaped into forms
enlightenment
range-finding vision
painting a world canvas
in different colours?

The life voyager's beacon

A driftwood fire
under grey skies
wind laced with harshly sour
salt-seasoned weed tang burns
flame dancing for voyagers
as the last sail
drops below the horizon
beyond a soul transition's
infinitely transitional
balance point
from which return
alone but forward
along the sun path
transcends
the fearsomely abyssal plunge
homing towards
a beacon blaze
daubed red/gold/white
across black night.

A love speculation

Perhaps love's dog collar
is the collar of service
fuelled by
heroically disturbed desire
to be desired,
in return for what?

Autumn equinox

The wind's calling card
for change irresistible
beyond nostalgia
for infinitely varied greens
impartial like justice
passes storm-driven sentence
on beach summers
green splendours
and brown hills
a whip, flail, scourer,
tidally cleaning
spring and summer's detritus
ransacking
memory's treasure chest
equally night and day
suspended
yet in motion
as cloud-harried skies
rusted falling leaves
and water flow's
stretto al fine
approach the seasonal coda.

Eleven

Sea images

Spun shadows weave light round a gull's short fluctuating glissando call.

*

Sea wind – restless sighing across seaweed lines tide stranded,

*

seabirds flock chattering soft discord smother above water/light interjections.

*

Wind-song spirit inhabits between tides, in flight sunwards.

*

Last sail drops below the horizon – an evening haunted beach.

*

Catch me sea smell, shell voice, birds sunset wind surfing towards fortress rising cliffs.

The image of touchdown

Trodden driveway gravel crunched
sea memories overriding
remembered routines
parading
holiday place nostalgia
where morning blackbirds
fluted challenges
to rapacious gulls
and a door opened onto mystery.

A haunting call echoed
cool slick breezes
over stark cliffs
whipping sea-pink falls
and a white bird's
long-flighted water touchdown
imaged in love
at a rock pool's tideline,
and infinitely cruising
sun tracking clouds
mirrored a present divide
between square-set familiarity
and variable infinities.

Commuters break the mould

In dislocated streams
we self-condition
to automated dreaming
self-enclosed
against meticulous monotony,
yet through innumerable
rush hour peregrinations
preserve fractured
remnant soul identities
masked by official resignation,
peel back
onion fashion
layered febrile consciousness
baring our complexly
unspoken desires
to resonate like crystal
exposing
secretly unselfish scenarios
for living
behind capital-encrusted
consumerised facades
while watching
swift-flown coruscating crowds
unravel under artificial light
as autonomous
integrated pilgrims
dreaming personal resurrection.

Australian landfalls

Into that brooding
continental stillness
at numerous landfalls
to confront the different mind
like unpolished stones
frictioned into newness
wind taxied…

some came shadow-taunted
seaward facing backed
by ancient speculative
wind/sun-eroded mass.

How, willingly
could the unwilling intimate
alien asymmetric forms
exiled complacently
by alien territorial tradition
at eye level confrontation
in impatient desire interpret
time-distended secrets?

Only when an age had wearied of itself
could they begin
to interact their dreams
with weather sculptured
sacred space reality's
silent-painted witnesses
be tipped
beyond immediacy's limited slip
into a different vision.

Winter solstice

Imaginary standstill
and the sun far gone
'St John-in-Winter'
heralds light's return
backtracking
through coming days
seeding hope
fire marked in festive mode
against winter night
illuminating
the World Tree
above/below rooted
in the Serpent's curled embrace
between sleep and waiting
dreaming spring.

Twelve

Migrant

'Leaving'…an echo of rebuke

turned from unspoken pressures
dark-suited coercive rituals
and gilded pages
I invoke magical distance
against certainties
between this moment, memories
glittering airport business currents
round islands of relaxation, unreal
as if observed from elsewhere
because of 'leaving'…echo

with inescapable imagery of voyaging
like muted drums resonant
across runways and parking bays
over quiescent leviathans
awaiting elemental calls to sail
through sky oceans
where the moon swims like a fish
caught on a gravity hook.

Evening, departure lounge phone calls
and greying beyond glass partitions…

I listen for the summons to relocation
returns conceptualised
down corridors of years
compromised

but 'leaving'…still echoes.

Afterwards I am turned
towards horizons of unavoidable knowledge.
Voices heard then
are beyond recall
'leaving'…an echo

I have not returned.

Perception of an echo

Smother-scatter waves
break into evening
on a breeze soft-spoken,
a subtly elemental
living resonance
echoing bird songs
haunting
the infinitesimal interval
of the echo perceived
in passing, leaving
like white foam in its wake
all things renounced,
recollection and release.

The Shell

Between tides
I select a shell
beige/white-banded
hinting red with serrated edges.

This abandoned
armoured microcosm of home
feels permanent yet is
at the ephemeral mercies of wind and tide
the same sand scourer
that foam wings whipped waves.

Sun squinting
I wonder what happened to its owner;
will our destinies
go similarly unrecorded?

Changes

Hesitation is
in the season's cusp
heat/cold alternating
competing, balancing.

The sun leaches green
for a bleached
burnt cream look
before stepping aside
for needle-thin showers.

Wind veers north, south
a warm blanket
a cold sheet.

Flowers come
and go like actors
flaunting yellow wattle
trumpetingly red bottle-brush.
Candy pink blossoms
are memories
blue dressed
jacaranda corps de ballet
making their entrance.

Encroaching heat
is desired on cold days
cursed when it come
Rain is wanted
in the dry
sun in the wet.

Disenchantment
reflects perhaps
premonitions of crisis
or just
the recurring cycle?

Spring Tides

No closure
in the gap between waves
a spring tide race
moon-wild
earth-turning power
is surf-rolling thunder
or the sea's artillery barrage
against eroding rocks…

and a disappearing splendour
with seaweed merely pushed
above familiar tidelines
driftwood cast up
to feed the fires of quest,
the sea retreats
spring passes
and is gone.

Epilogue

The sun behind the sun

Time through running
the sun behind the sun
is a fire in the rose
flaming
'back to the future'
forward to the past
under a white clear
sunrise revelation's
presently timeless moment
lightning-like racing
crossing over
through dreams time free
going and coming
simultaneously.

The scapegoat
has no destiny
beyond sins offloaded
onto innocence
pre-figuring
the Sun behind the Sun
confined
to knocking on a handle-less door,
yet desert death
before a merciless barrier
of burning hills
releases the Sun
behind the Sun to shine
unshadowed
rebirthing
for the fire and the rose.

www.ingramcontent.com/pod-product-compliance
Lightning Source LLC
Chambersburg PA
CBHW070943080526
44589CB00013B/1618